ADVENTURE S

SKIING and SNOW SPORTS

Jackie Gaff and David Jefferis

Kingfisher Books

Text consultant:
Howard Bass

Illustrated by:
Drawing Attention
James Robins

Photographs supplied by:
Action Plus
All Sport
Tony Henshaw
Rob Jewell
David Jefferis
Charles Kerry

**With special thanks to
Lillywhites Ltd, London,
for lending the equipment
on the cover.**

Kingfisher Books, Grisewood & Dempsey Ltd,
Elsley House, 24–30 Great Titchfield Street,
London W1P 7AD.

First published in 1989 by Kingfisher Books

Copyright © Grisewood & Dempsey Ltd 1989

BRITISH LIBRARY CATALOGUING IN PUBLICATION DATA
Gaff, Jackie
   Skiing and snow sports
   1. Snow sports – For children
   I. Title   II. Jefferis, David   III. Series
   796.9
ISBN 0 86272 415 5

All rights reserved. No part of this publication
may be reproduced, stored in a retrieval system
or transmitted by any means, electronic, mechanical,
photocopying or otherwise, without the prior
permission of the publisher.

Phototypeset by Southern Positives and Negatives (SPAN),
Lingfield, Surrey
Printed in Spain

Contents

Heading for the snow   4

EQUIPMENT
Dressed for the slopes   6
Downhill skis and bindings   8
Cross-country skiing   10

DOWNHILL BASICS
First day on the slopes   12
The quickest way down   14
Slipping and sliding   16
Turning and falling   18

AT HOME ON THE SNOW
Ticket to ride   20
Skiing with confidence   22

COMPETITION SKIING
The first skiers   24
Downhill and slalom   26
Ski jumping   28
Freestyle action   30

OTHER SNOW SPORTS
Cresting new waves   32
Built for speed   34

Cameras for the ski slopes   36
Glossary   38
Index   40

Heading for the snow

■ The first snowfall of winter is magical, as is making the first footprint on that spotless white covering. Carving the first ski trail into a mountainside freshly coated with new snow is even more exhilarating – and only a holiday and a few ski lessons away.

There are two different branches to the sport. Skiing down mountains is called alpine or downhill. The other type of skiing is close to walking and is called nordic or cross-country.

▶ Alpine racing is only for the experienced – just watching the speed and grace of these skiers takes the breath away!

▼ The start of a cross-country race. Sometimes, hundreds of contestants take part in these nordic events.

EQUIPMENT

Dressed for the slopes

■ The correct equipment is very important when you go skiing. It is expensive to buy, but nearly everything you need can be hired from ski shops at home or at your holiday resort.

Clothes must fit comfortably and keep you warm and dry. They should also let you move around easily, as you'll be doing a lot of bending and stretching once you hit the slopes.

Ready for action!

Ski suits come in a confusing range of styles and colours, but all you really need for outer wear are an anorak, trousers and gloves – all of them windproof and snowproof. Gaps around the waist let in snow and cold air, so many people wear one-piece suits or the high-waisted ski dungarees called salopettes. A woollen hat will stop you losing body heat through the top of your head.

It's best to have layers of clothes underneath the ski suit, as the air trapped between them will be heated by your body and keep it warm.

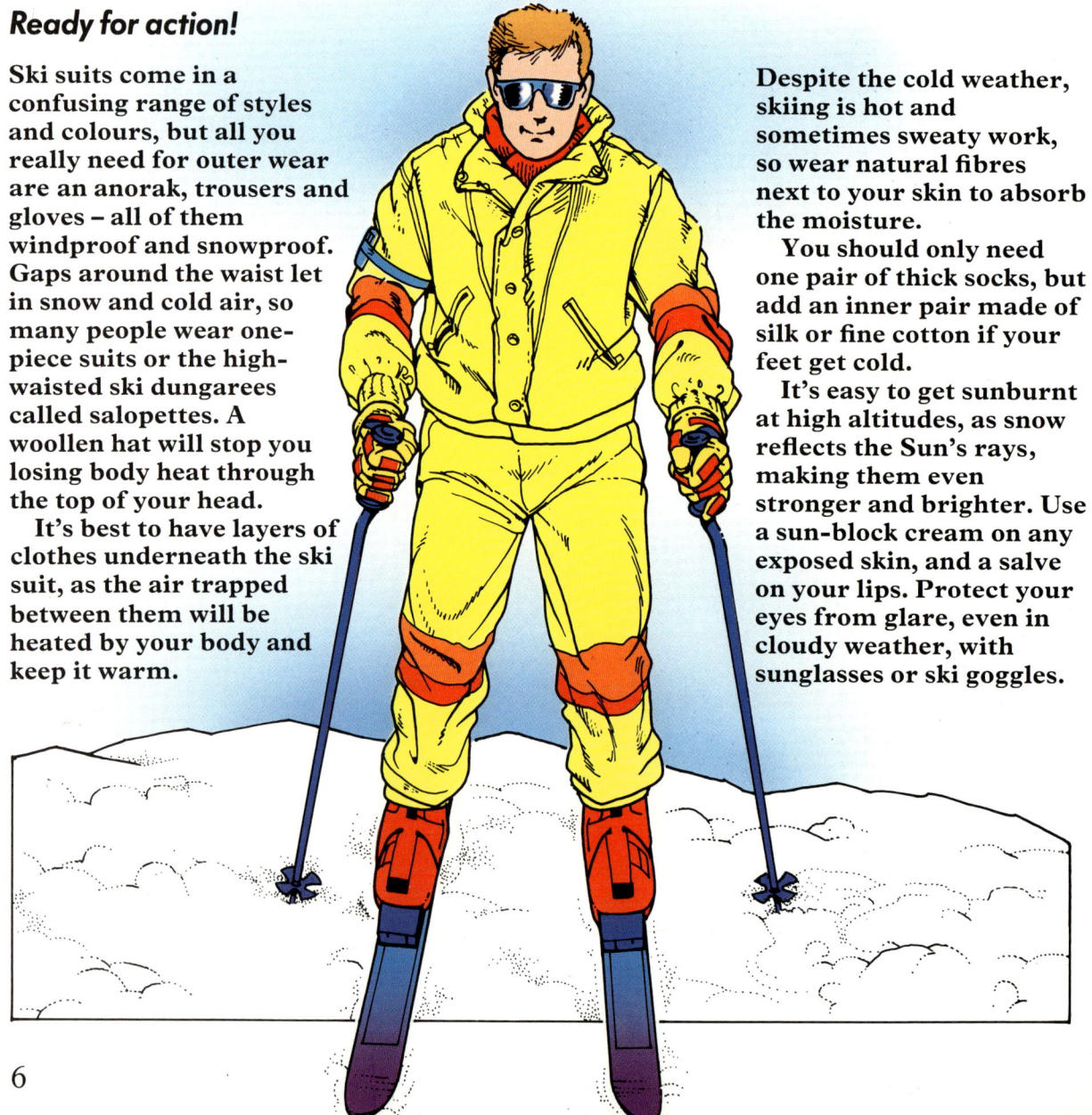

Despite the cold weather, skiing is hot and sometimes sweaty work, so wear natural fibres next to your skin to absorb the moisture.

You should only need one pair of thick socks, but add an inner pair made of silk or fine cotton if your feet get cold.

It's easy to get sunburnt at high altitudes, as snow reflects the Sun's rays, making them even stronger and brighter. Use a sun-block cream on any exposed skin, and a salve on your lips. Protect your eyes from glare, even in cloudy weather, with sunglasses or ski goggles.

Best foot forward

Boots support your ankles, protecting them from sprains and breaks, so they must fit closely. Your heel and ankle must be held firmly, but the boots mustn't pinch your feet. You should be able to wiggle your toes and bend your ankle forwards, but you shouldn't be able to lift your heel.

◀ Boots are made of plastic, foam and fabric.
1. An adjustable clip closes the boot – different settings make it tighter or looser.
2. Rear-entry boots open at the heel.
3. Some boots have a dial or a lever at the back, which is used to adjust the fit over the instep.
4. Another lever or dial controls the fit around the toes.

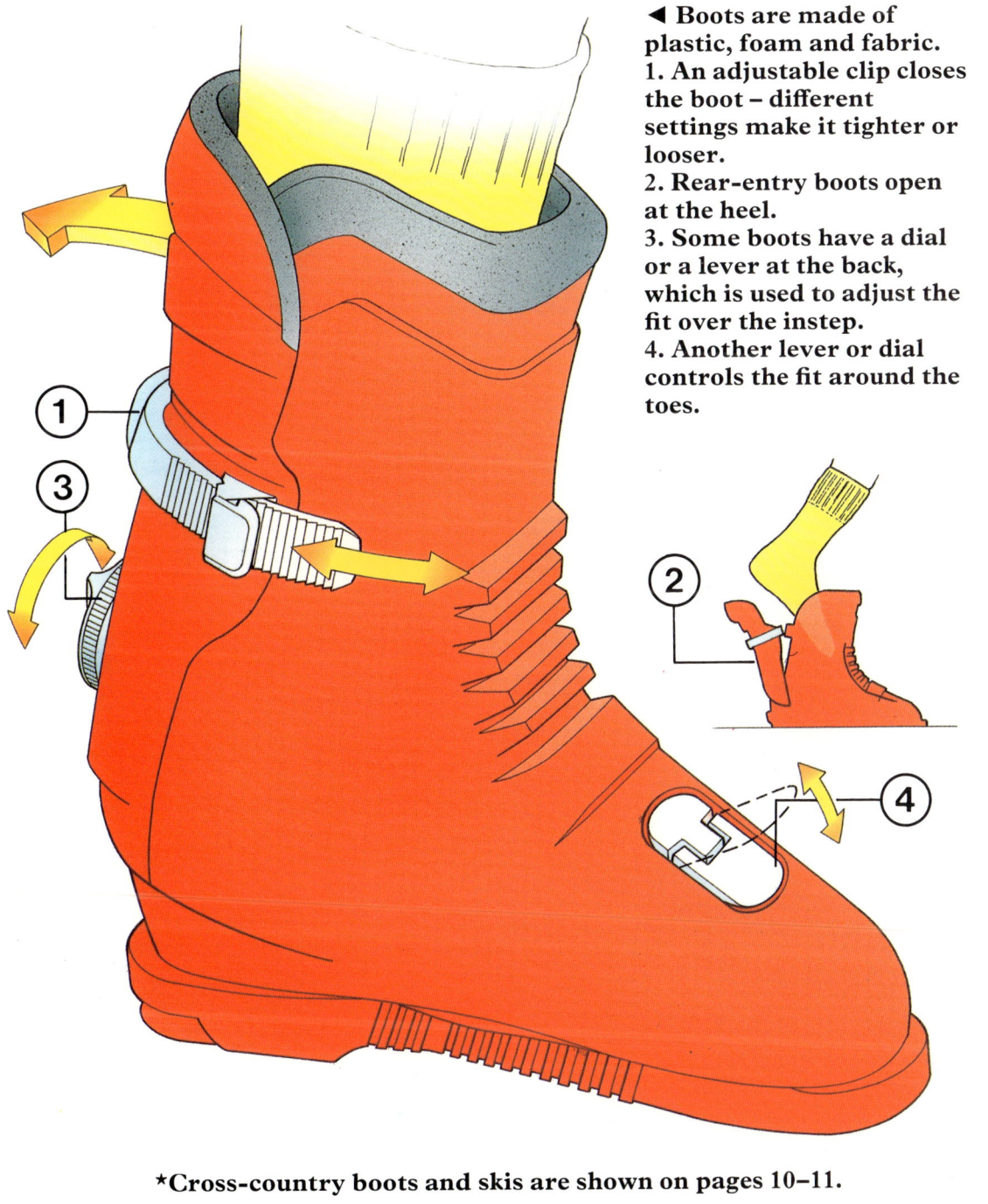

*Cross-country boots and skis are shown on pages 10–11.

EQUIPMENT

Downhill skis and bindings

■ Bindings are metal fittings which clasp the toe and heel of the boot, attaching it to the ski. Set properly, they will release the boot from the ski if you fall awkwardly, so that you don't injure your legs. Have them set by an expert when you buy or hire your equipment.

Skis come in different lengths, depending on height, skiing experience and snow conditions – once again, get professional advice. Long skis help with balance at speed, but short skis turn more easily. Beginners often start on short skis and gradually build up to full-length ones.

▲ Ski poles help you to balance and turn. Put your hand through the loop of the strap, then grasp it and the handle, with your thumb over the loop.

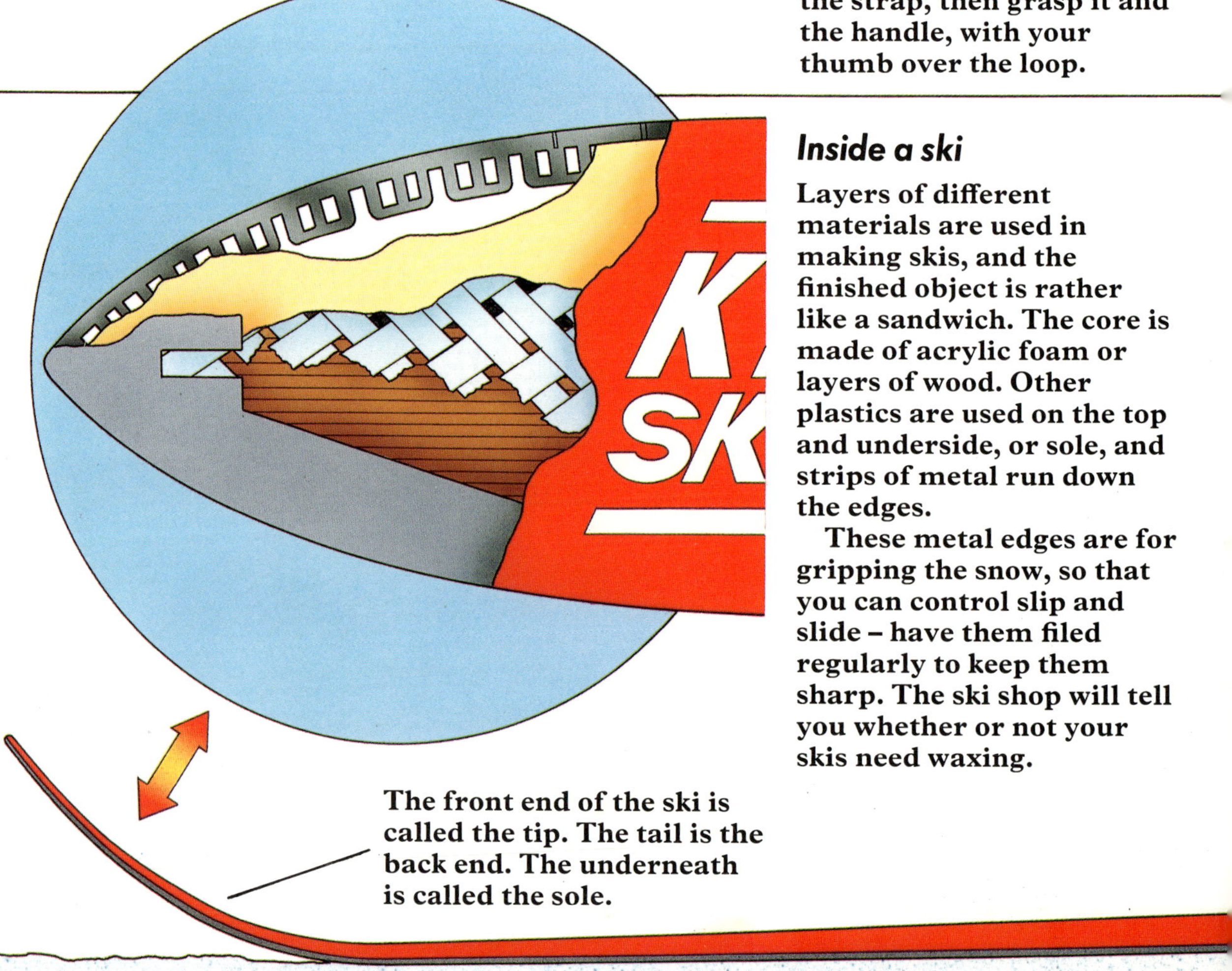

Inside a ski

Layers of different materials are used in making skis, and the finished object is rather like a sandwich. The core is made of acrylic foam or layers of wood. Other plastics are used on the top and underside, or sole, and strips of metal run down the edges.

These metal edges are for gripping the snow, so that you can control slip and slide – have them filed regularly to keep them sharp. The ski shop will tell you whether or not your skis need waxing.

The front end of the ski is called the tip. The tail is the back end. The underneath is called the sole.

8

Standing on skis

Balance is very important on skis – lose it and you'll fall over! The key is the way you hold your body.

Stand on flat ground with your legs and feet slightly apart and your weight evenly balanced on the balls of both feet. Keeping your upper body straight and your bottom tucked in, lean forward against the front of your boots and bend your knees.

Try to relax! Flex your knees a little – when you start skiing, they will act as your body's shock absorbers, soaking up the bumps.

Lean forwards against your boots

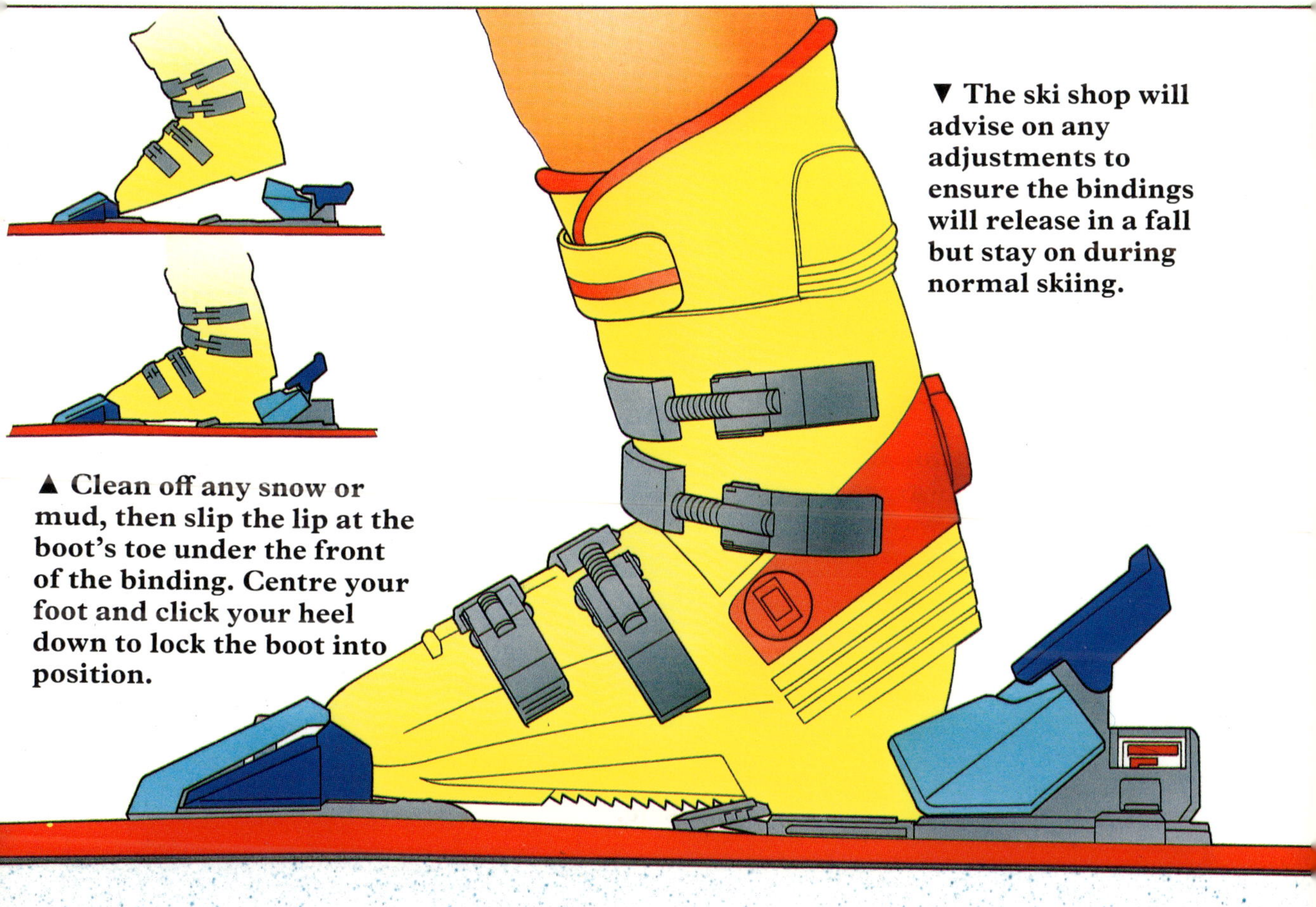

Don't stick your bottom out!

▼ The ski shop will advise on any adjustments to ensure the bindings will release in a fall but stay on during normal skiing.

▲ Clean off any snow or mud, then slip the lip at the boot's toe under the front of the binding. Centre your foot and click your heel down to lock the boot into position.

EQUIPMENT

Cross-country skiing

■ Nordic or cross-country equipment is designed to allow skiers to walk uphill and across land, as well as skiing downhill. The movement for cross-country skiing is similar to walking, which can't be done comfortably keeping the heels flat on the ground. To allow for this, the bindings on cross-country skis only grip the toe of the boot – the heel lifts free of the ski with each stride.

► There's no need for special clothes when cross-country skiing, as long as you are warm and can move freely. Because wet snow-covered trousers are so uncomfortable flapping around the ankles, many nordic skiers wear knee-length breeches.

Boots and skis

Cross-country boots are rather like trainers and very different to the clumpy ones worn for downhill skiing. The boot shown on the right covers and supports the ankle, but low-cut boots are worn for racing.

Nordic skis are narrower and lighter than alpine ones. So that the skier glides forwards, but doesn't slide back, the soles of the skis are specially treated. Each ski has gliding zones front and back, and a gripping zone in the middle. The soles of some nordic skis are treated with wax, and there are special waxes for gliding and others for gripping.

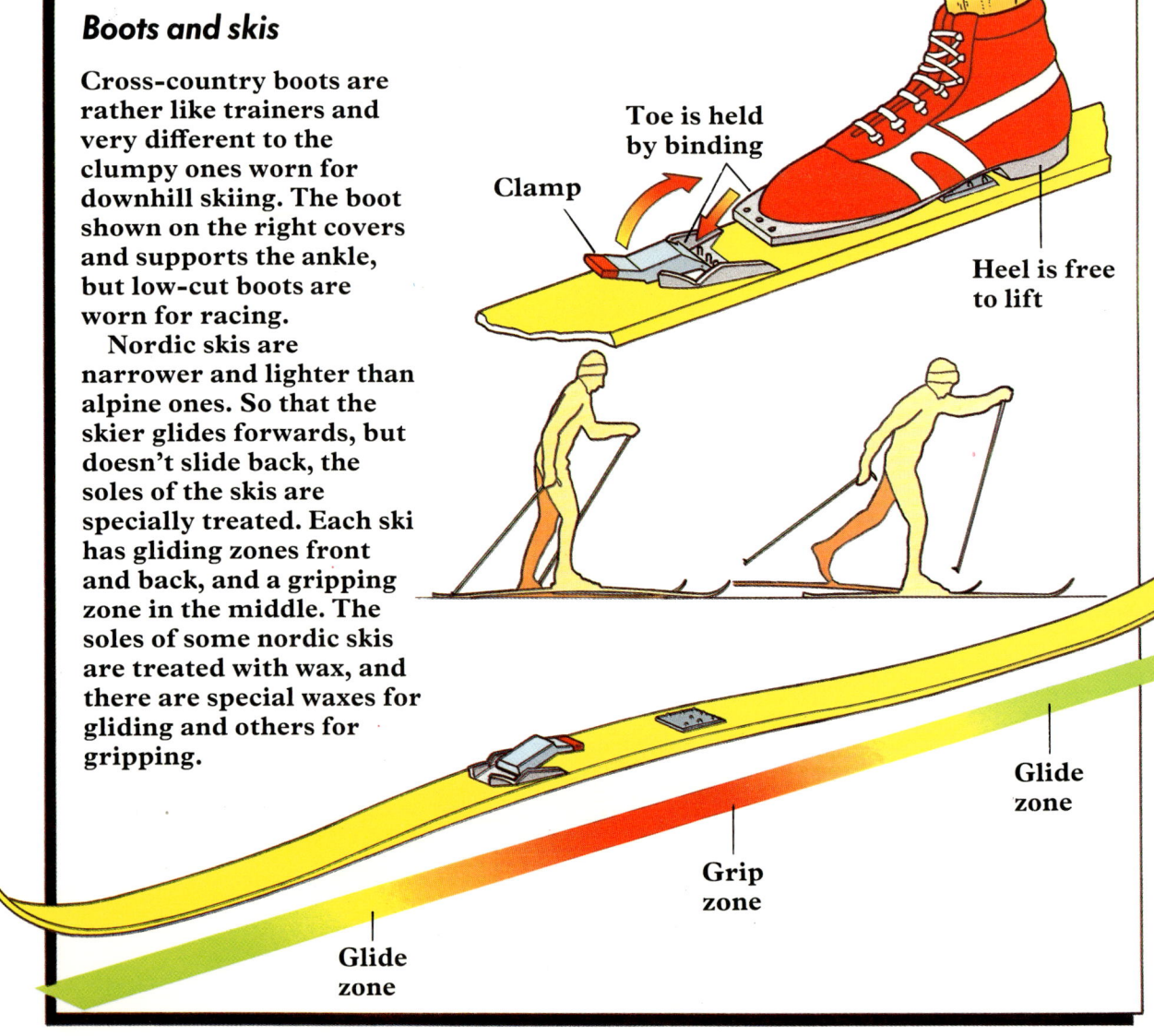

DOWNHILL BASICS

First day on the slopes

■ The first time you put your boots and skis on you'll probably wonder how you'll ever be able to move on the flat, let alone ski gracefully down a hill. Don't worry – you'll be amazed at how quickly you learn to balance, glide and turn on those plank-like objects.

You'll learn fastest, and stay safest, if you take lessons from a qualified instructor. Most resorts have ski schools – if you book morning lessons, you can practise with friends in the afternoons.

▶ Ski schools offer lessons to individuals or groups, but it's more expensive to learn on your own and easier to make friends in a group.

8. Fall over . . .

9. . . . and learn how to get up again!

7. Herringbone up slope

6. Schuss down

5. Sidestep up slope

1. Carry skis to nursery slopes

2. Put on skis

3. Check stance

4. Learn to walk

First lessons

It won't take you long to relax and feel comfortable on skis. Beginners' areas are often called nursery slopes, and they have very gentle gradients. You'll put on your skis on the flat and get used to walking around on them – put your weight on one ski and slide the opposite one forwards. Try to keep your skis parallel and hip-width apart, and don't cross your tips or tails!

You'll also learn how to climb slopes, so that you can try straight downhill running, called schussing.

Falling can be a useful way of stopping when you're a beginner. There's a correct way to do it if you want to avoid injury (see page 19) – it also makes getting up again a lot easier!

Herringbone

This is one way of climbing a hill on skis, but because it's hard work herringboning is best used on gentle slopes.

Face uphill, with your skis in a V-shape, and push your knees inwards to grip the snow with the skis' inside edges. Take one step at a time, edging hard. Use your poles for support and balance.

Sidestep

Do this to climb steeper slopes. Stand with your skis together, side-on to the hill so that you don't slide forwards or backwards. Push your knees forwards and sideways into the hill to edge your skis and grip the snow. Step up one ski at a time – top ski, then bottom ski – always edging your weighted ski hard into the snow.

DOWNHILL BASICS

The quickest way down

■ The shortest and most direct route down a slope is called the fall line. And the quickest way to ski the fall line is a straight downhill run. This type of run is called a schuss – the word means 'shot' in German – and on gentle slopes it is easy for beginners to master. Stopping and turning are another matter, of course, and for these you'll need to learn how to snowplough.

▼ In skiing, the fall line is the straightest way down a slope. It will vary, depending on where you are on the mountain, so use your eyes to tell you which way to go.

▼ On gentle slopes you can either schuss like the skier on the right, or snowplough like the skier in the foreground. Always make sure you are leaning forwards properly – these skiers are both standing too upright.

14

The snowplough

This technique will add control to your skiing, and enable you to slow down and stop. You'll also use it for turning (see page 18). To slow down, bend your knees and sink a little as you push your heels out. This will shift your weight to your skis' inner edges, making them grip and act as brakes. Sinking lower and pushing your heels out harder will make you stop.

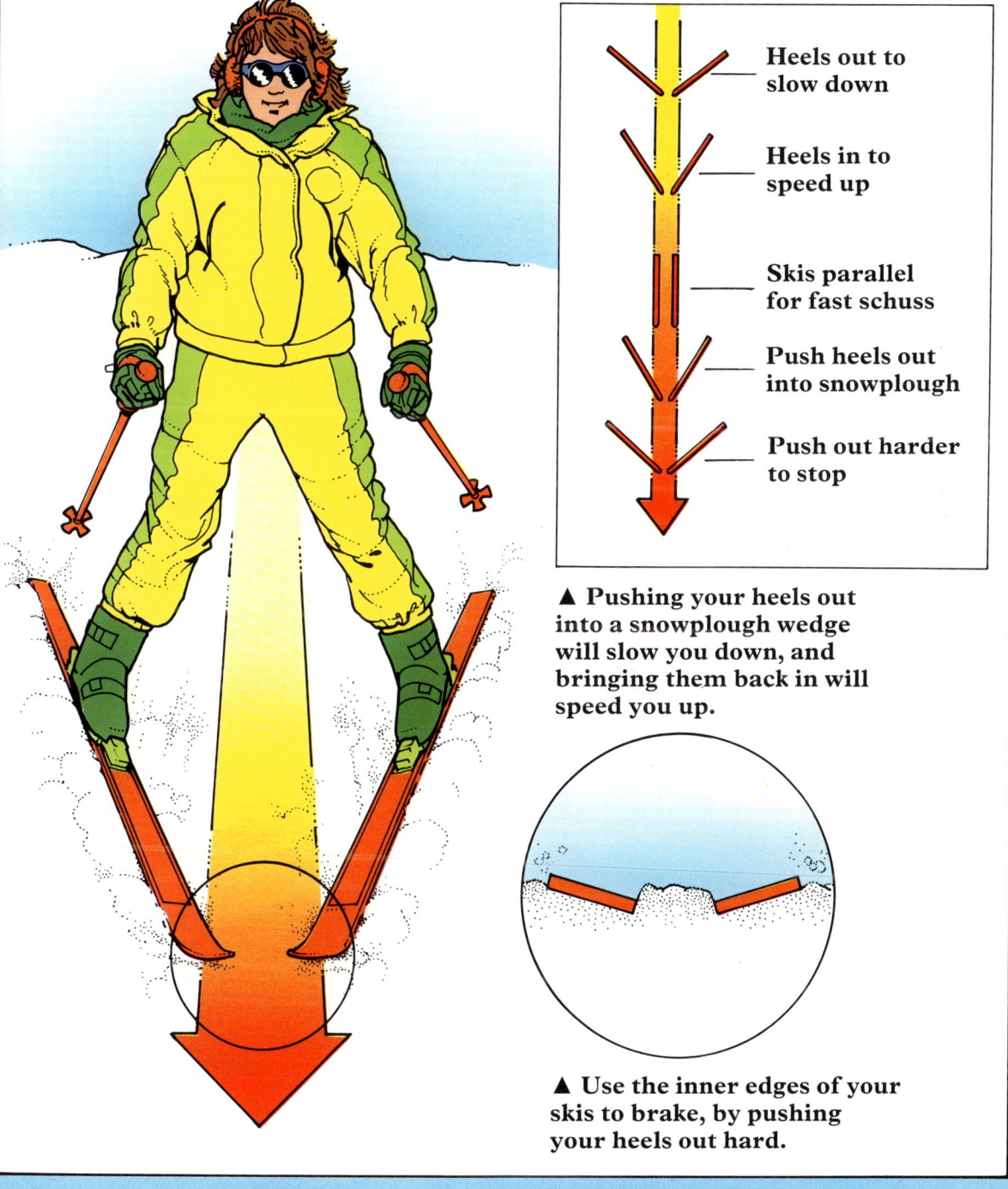

- Heels out to slow down
- Heels in to speed up
- Skis parallel for fast schuss
- Push heels out into snowplough
- Push out harder to stop

▲ Pushing your heels out into a snowplough wedge will slow you down, and bringing them back in will speed you up.

▲ Use the inner edges of your skis to brake, by pushing your heels out hard.

15

DOWNHILL BASICS

Slipping and sliding

■ Although schussing down the fall line is a fun way to tackle gentle slopes, on steep hills it's far too fast for beginners. The best way to cope with most slopes is to ski across them. This is called traversing and it demands a special body position – knees and hips pushing into the slope, and upper body facing downhill and bending outwards slightly from the waist.

◀ Try to keep your skis fairly close together when traversing. Put most of your weight on the lower ski and let the upper one ride gently across the snow – the upper ski should be slightly in front. In order to stay on track and not slip downhill, you'll have to grip with your skis' uphill edges. To do this, and to balance, bend like a banana – knees and hips into the slope, upper body facing down and out.

Sideslip

Use this to avoid any obstacles. Straighten your knees until you release your edges and your skis flatten. You'll start to slip downhill. Push your knees into the slope again to edge your skis and stop.

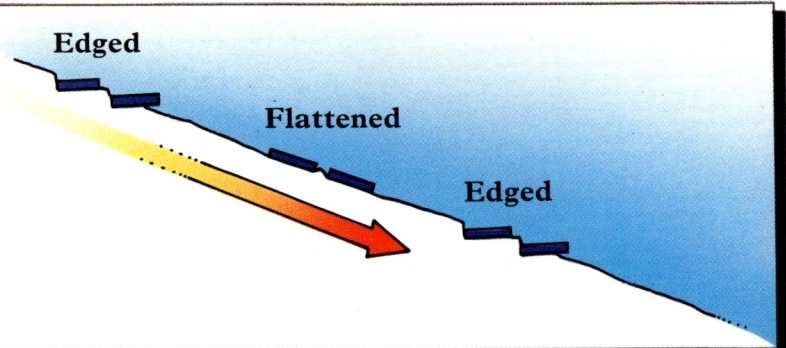

▲ The angle of your traverse will determine your speed. The closer you ski to the fall line, the faster you'll go.

▶ These machines are used to prepare ski runs and keep them safe by smoothing out ruts and bumps. They're called piste-makers, because at ski resorts the runs are called pistes.

DOWNHILL BASICS

Turning and falling

■ Steering your way down a mountain depends on your ability to turn – the more skilled you become at turning, the more control you'll have over direction and speed.

There are a few different ski turns, and beginners usually start with the snowplough. Whatever the turn, let your feet and knees do the work – don't twist from the shoulders or hips.

Snowplough turn

In the snowplough wedge, ski down the fall line of a gentle slope. Your weight should be evenly balanced on your skis' inner edges. Now sink a little at the knees and push out your right ski. This will shift your weight to your right ski and you'll turn left.

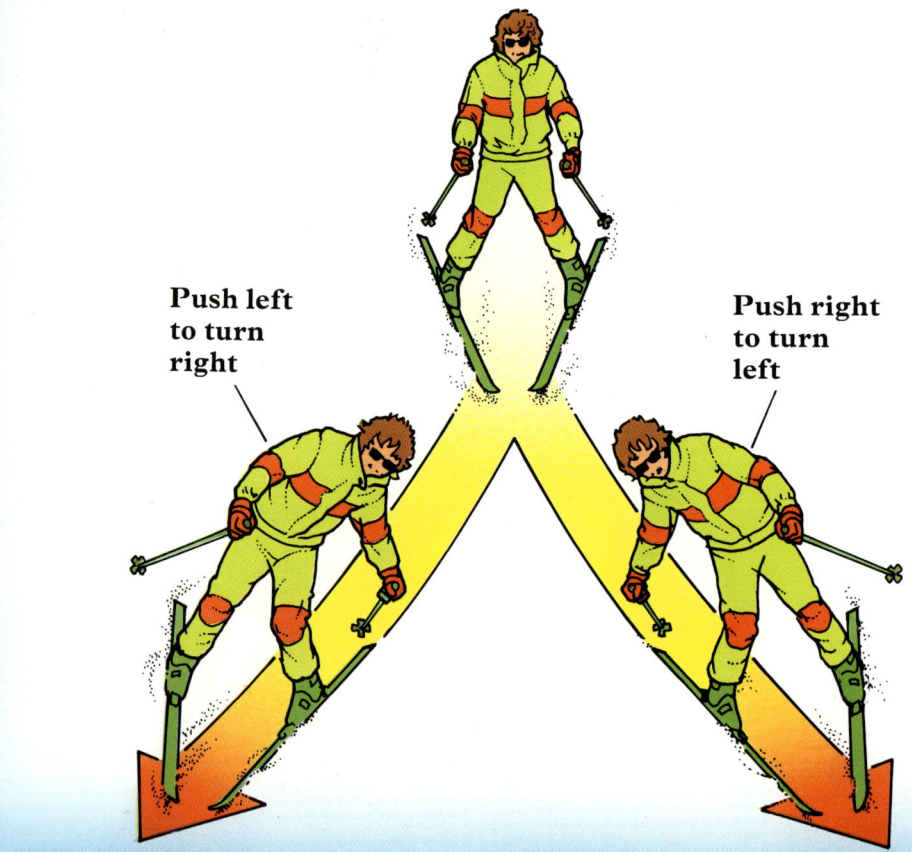

Push left to turn right

Push right to turn left

Stem turn

With your body in the banana position, traverse the fall line of a gentle slope. The steeper your traverse, the faster you'll go and the easier it will be to turn. Push your heels out into the snowplough wedge, then continue pushing the tail of your upper ski out further to start a turn. As you come round, rise up slightly and slide or step your lighter ski (the old lower one) in parallel to your weighted ski (the old upper one). Sink down again, and edge your skis for the next traverse.

▶ All skiers will fall sometimes, even those with years and years of experience. Practise the correct way to do it, and remember that you are even less likely to hurt yourself if you relax! It's best to fall into the slope, your body up and your legs down. Straighten your legs as you fall, and sit on the slope above your skis. Keep your hands up and in front of your body and hold your poles firmly – this will protect fingers and thumbs.

Make sure your skis are at right angles to the fall line before you try to get up, so that you don't slip away downhill before you are ready. Draw your skis up towards you, plant your poles behind and beside you, then push.

Skis at right angle to fall line

19

AT HOME ON THE SNOW

Ticket to ride

■ You'll discover all sorts of ways to get to the top of the runs at your ski resort, but before you get on any of the lifts you'll need to buy a ski pass. Like season tickets, ski passes are issued for varying lengths of time. You won't want to fumble in your pockets for your pass every time you catch a lift – or risk dropping it – so fix it to the chest or sleeve of your ski jacket.

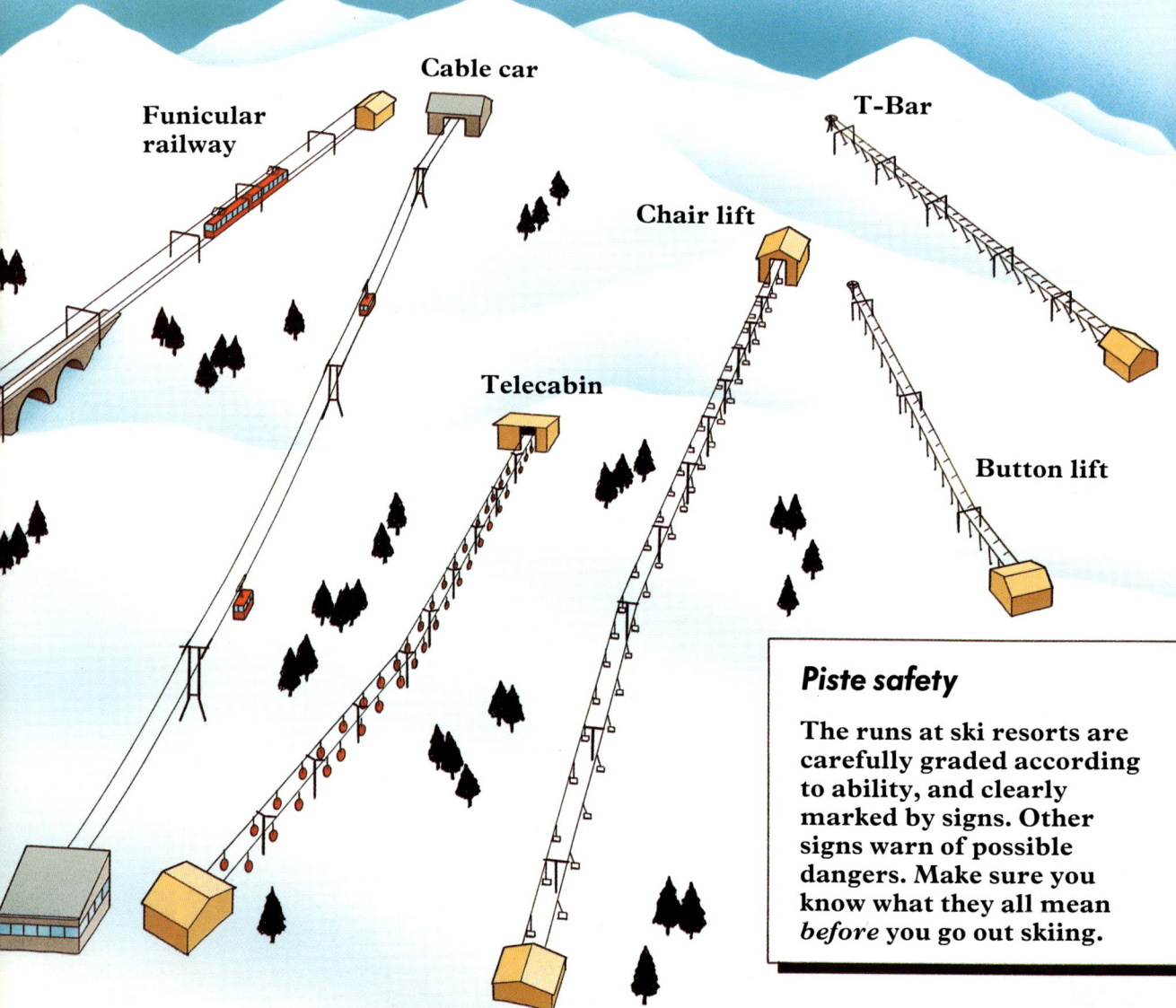

Piste safety

The runs at ski resorts are carefully graded according to ability, and clearly marked by signs. Other signs warn of possible dangers. Make sure you know what they all mean *before* you go out skiing.

▶ Telecabins seat two to four people inside, with their skis and poles in special racks beside the doors. The spidery metal towers suspend the steel cables above the snowy mountainsides.

Very easy (okay for beginners) | Easy piste (medium in USA)  | Medium piste (Europe)  | Difficult (advanced skiers only) | Danger | Piste closed | Avalanche danger (piste closed)

AT HOME ON THE SNOW

Skiing with confidence

■ As you become more experienced, you'll learn techniques for dealing with the steeper pistes and for skiing at speed. You'll also begin to feel – and look – more graceful!

One way of skiing faster is to make the body more streamlined. For a fast schuss, crouch down into the egg position – arms and knees forward over the skis, with poles tucked up and back.

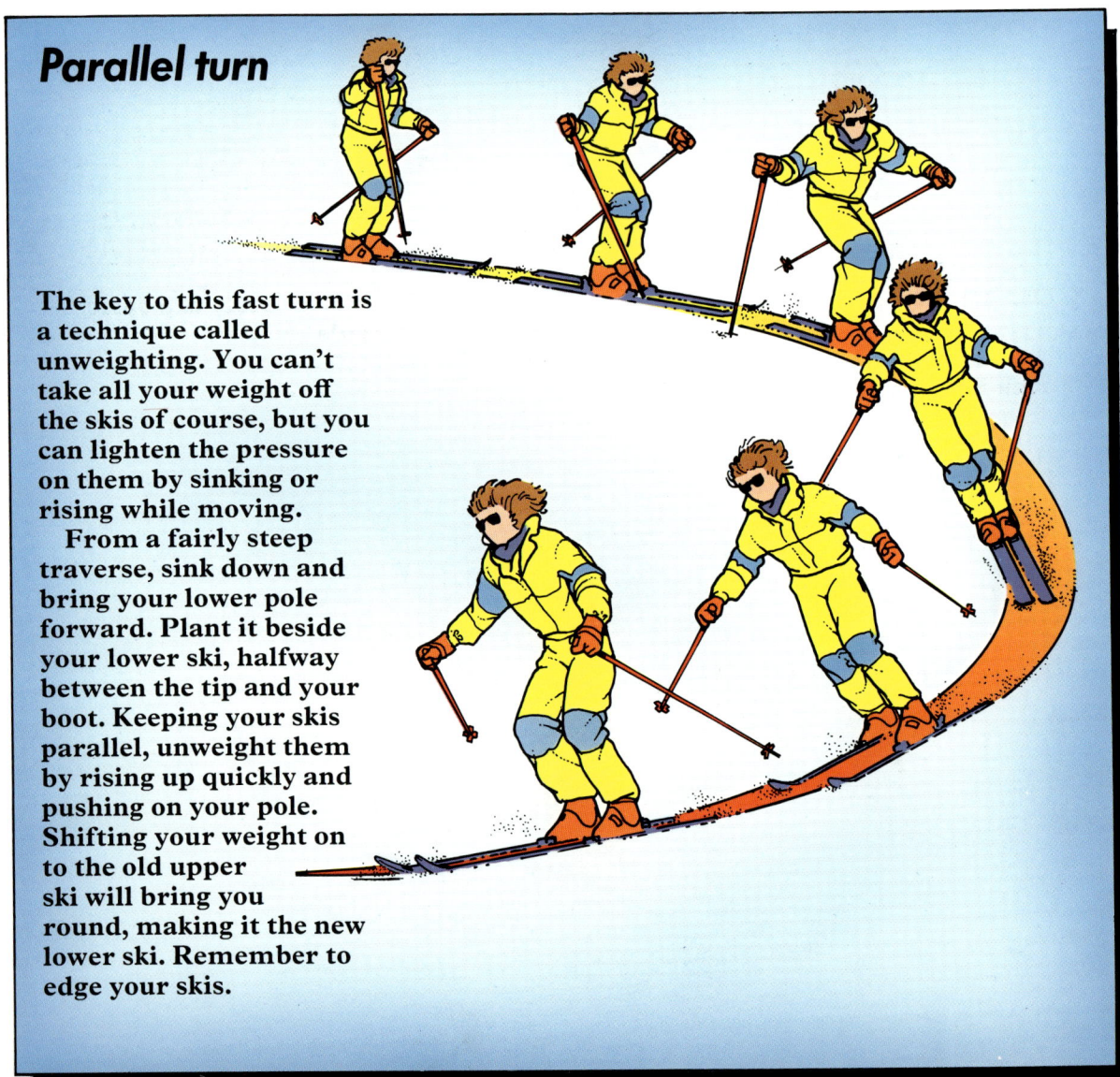

Parallel turn

The key to this fast turn is a technique called unweighting. You can't take all your weight off the skis of course, but you can lighten the pressure on them by sinking or rising while moving.

From a fairly steep traverse, sink down and bring your lower pole forward. Plant it beside your lower ski, halfway between the tip and your boot. Keeping your skis parallel, unweight them by rising up quickly and pushing on your pole. Shifting your weight on to the old upper ski will bring you round, making it the new lower ski. Remember to edge your skis.

Snow sense

The greatest danger on the slopes comes from out-of-control skiers. They risk hurting themselves and other people as they crash and bash their way downwards. You'll stay safer and have more fun if you know what your limitations as a skier are, and act within them.

▲ Don't be careless when carrying your skis – you could easily hit someone, or even knock them out cold.

▲ Never ski alone. Go with a friend, so that there's someone to fetch help if one of you is injured.

▲ The skiing code of rules gives the right of way to the skier in front. Remember this when overtaking other skiers.

▼ Ski safely is a basic rule – and this can extend to equipment. Here, beginners wear lightweight helmets.

23

COMPETITION SKIING

The first skiers

■ Skiing began over 4000 years ago, as a way of travelling cross-country in the snowy regions of northern Europe. We know this because skiers are depicted in rock carvings which date from that time. Prehistoric skis have also been discovered. They were made from wood, as were all skis right up to the 1920s.

Ski schools and resorts, and most of the downhill skiing techniques, have only developed in the last 100 or so years. The world's first ski clubs were the Trysil Club of Norway and the Kiandra Club of Australia, both founded in the 1860s. The first ski school opened in the early 1880s in Telemark, Norway.

▼ Early skiers wore wooden skis and used a single wooden pole for steering, like these 19th-century Australians skiing in the Snowy Mountains.

Competitive skiing

The world's first ski races were held in Norway and Australia in the 1850s and 1860s. Today the main skiing competitions are the Olympics, the World Championships, and the World Cup. Modern alpine events cover downhill and slalom races, while cross-country races and ski jumping are classed as nordic events.

The first World Championships were held in 1925, for cross-country racing, and the first alpine events took place in 1931, at Mürren, in Switzerland. They are now held every two years.

The inaugural Winter Olympics were held in Chamonix, in the French Alps, in 1924, but alpine events were not included until 1936. Nowadays the Winter Olympics include 13 or so snow sports and normally take place every four years.

The World Cup began in 1967. It is held every year and lasts most of the winter, as skiers compete in a succession of alpine events.

*Winter Olympics will be held in 1992 and 1994 so that in future they will take place halfway between the Summer Olympics, and not in the same year.

◂ Slalom is a downhill skiing race over a winding course, which is marked out by sets of poles called gates.

25

COMPETITION SKIING

Downhill and slalom

■ The fastest of the competitive skiing events, and the most dangerous, is downhill racing. The courses are around 3 kilometres long and very steep, with drops of 800–1000 metres for men and 500–700 metres for women.

Slalom events test skill in turning, as competitors have to weave around and between sets of poles called gates.

▶ With streamlined clothes and equipment, skiers can reach speeds of over 200 km/h in a straight downhill schuss, their bodies in the classic egg position. The official downhill speed trial is called the flying kilometre.

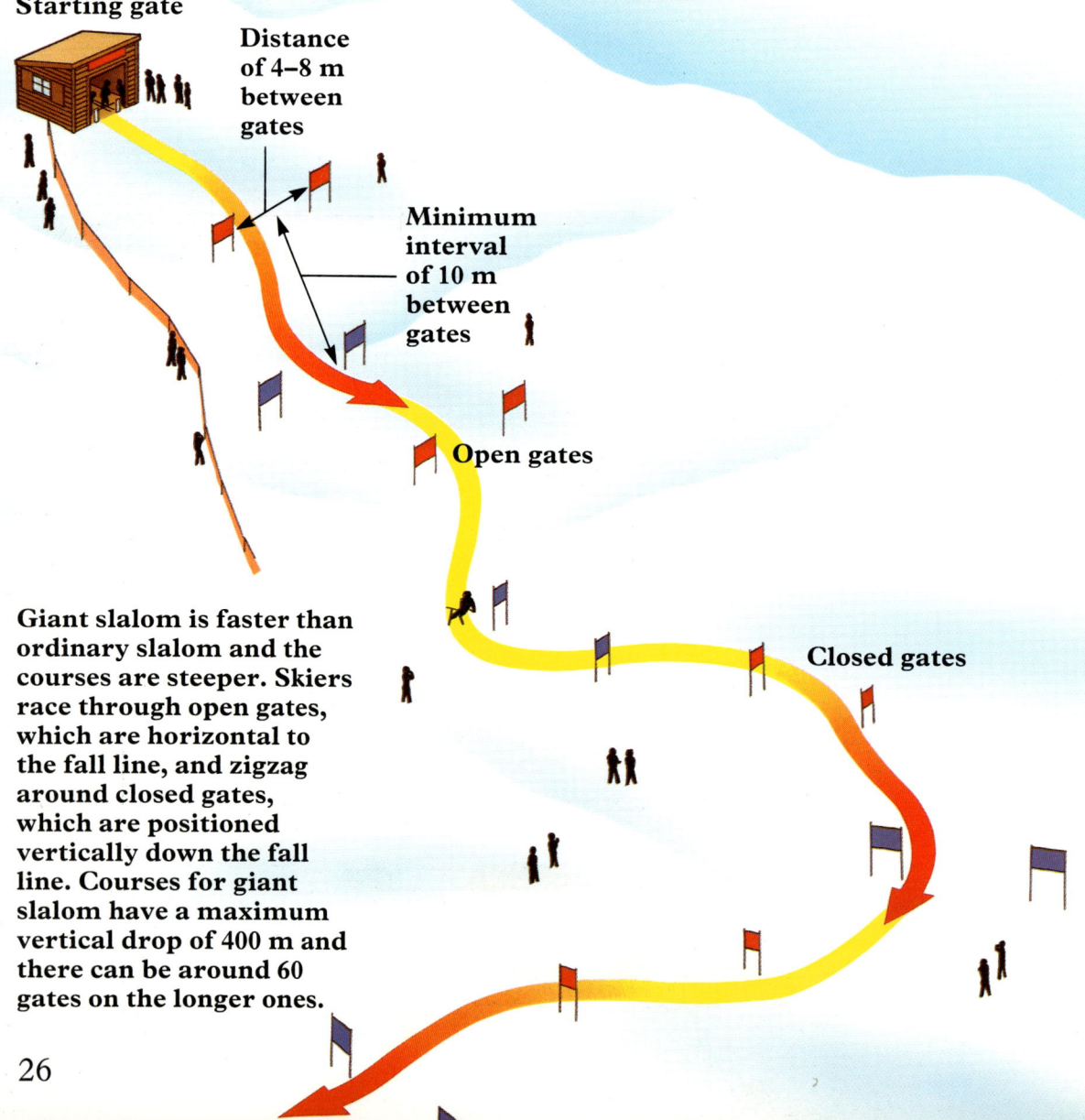

Giant slalom is faster than ordinary slalom and the courses are steeper. Skiers race through open gates, which are horizontal to the fall line, and zigzag around closed gates, which are positioned vertically down the fall line. Courses for giant slalom have a maximum vertical drop of 400 m and there can be around 60 gates on the longer ones.

COMPETITION SKIING

Ski jumping

■ There are various competitions in this spectacular nordic event, and in most of them points are awarded for style and body position as well as for the length of the jump.

Competitors wear specially adapted cross-country skis, which are longer, wider and heavier than usual. Grooves in the soles help the ski jumpers to steer – unless they are airborne!

◀ A skier swoops down the in-run, accelerating to jumping speed in a few seconds.

In-run ramp

▶ Jumpers lean forward to get maximum lift while in the air. Skis must be parallel and poles are not used.

Competitions involving the longest jumps – distances greater than 90 m – are aptly named ski flying and results are determined purely on distance covered.

The jump

Very steep ramps, called in-runs, help skiers to build fast takeoff speeds for their jumps.
1. The skier races down the in-run in the streamlined egg position.
2. At takeoff the skier jumps out of the crouch and leans forward.
3. Body and skis are kept as streamlined as possible.
4. The skier lands with arms outstretched for balance, knees bent to absorb the shock of hitting the ground.

The landing slope has coloured lines to make jumps safer. It is dangerous to land beyond the critical point.

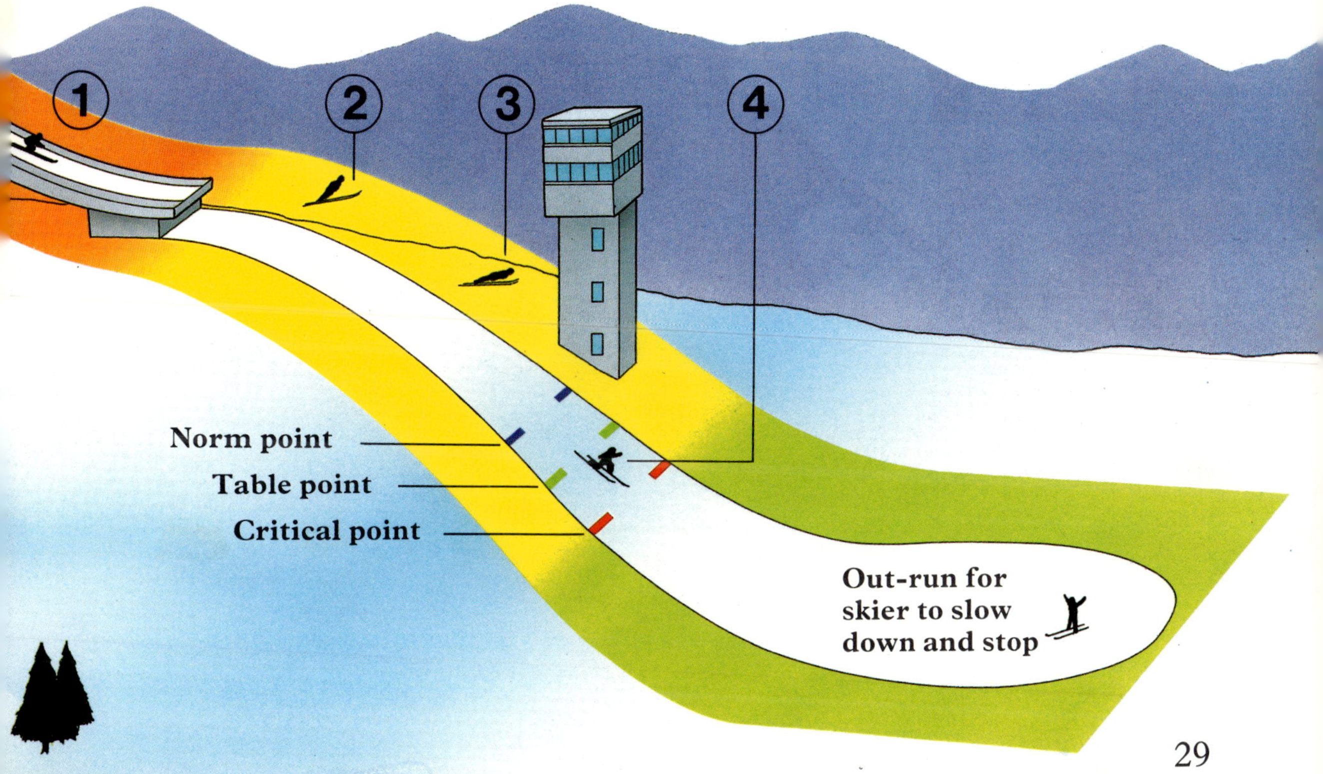

Norm point
Table point
Critical point

Out-run for skier to slow down and stop

29

COMPETITION SKIING

Freestyle action

■ Skiing continues to develop as a sport, as people experiment and stretch their skills to the limit. Freestyle started in the late 1960s, when skiers began inventing sensational stunts and acrobatics.

There are three different forms of freestyle – aerials, ballet and mogul – and short skis are worn for all of them. Aerials are probably the most dramatic. Skiers launch themselves off a short ramp and perform a range of jumps and somersaults while airborne.

▶ Aerial skiers don't limit themselves to single somersaults – with a steep ramp they can manage doubles and even triples.

◀ The short ramp used for aerials is called a kicker. Aerials are the most dangerous of the freestyle forms, and skiers train very carefully before trying out difficult or new manoeuvres on the snow. Trampolines are often used for practice sessions, or a ramp is set up over a swimming pool so that the skier isn't injured by an awkward landing.

OTHER SNOW SPORTS

Cresting new waves

■ The latest sport to hit the slopes combines skiing with surfing and skateboarding techniques. It's called snowboarding, and skiers balance on one fat ski instead of two thin ones. Besides their own alpine and freestyle events, snowboarders have a special competition which they've developed from skateboarding. Halfpipes are sloping troughs made of snow, with high sidewalls which snowboarders ride like frozen waves – shooting up and flying off into the air.

▼ Snowboarders stand side-on to their board, unlike other mono-skiers whose feet are in the usual skiing position. Keeping their front knee bent, snowboarders lean forwards from the hips and use their back foot to steer – kicking it forwards to turn right and backwards to turn left.

Shredspeak...

...or how to sound rad on a shred sled! Here is a mini-dictionary of snowboarding language.

Bail – fall, wipeout
Chillin' out – resting
Dialed – mastered
Ducks – skiers
Dude – a fellow snowboarder
Goofy foot – right foot forward on the board
Killer – very good
Nose roll – circular spin balanced on board tip
Rad (radical) – cool, outstanding
Rocket air – grabbing board tip in mid-air
Shred – to ride well
Shred sled – snowboard
Stoked – excited

▲ If you really want to put your feet up, try dog-sled racing! Standing on the back of the sled, drivers use harness and whip to control a team of husky racers.

▼ When you're bored with surfing, you might like to try waterskiing on the snow! Skijoring (from the Norwegian for 'ski-driving') lets the horse take the strain.

OTHER SNOW SPORTS

Built for speed

■ Although you can do it sitting or lying down, sledging is as fast and demanding as all the other downhill snow sports. Besides the bobsleigh pictured below, the other main type of racing sledge is the luge. This is basically a seat slung between two sharp metal runners. Riders lie back and hold on to a strap attached to the front of the runners, leaning their bodies to steer.

▼ Bobsleighs are built for crews of four, as well as for two. They have two sets of runners – at the front and at the back – and a brake for emergencies. The pilot steers by turning the front runners with a rope or a steering wheel.

▶ One of the world's most famous sledging courses is the Cresta Run, at St Moritz in Switzerland. It's over 1 km long, and one-person sledges called skeletons are used. These have a metal frame with a lightweight sliding platform on which the rider lies – moving forwards increases speed, sliding back slows you down.

▼ Speeds of over 125 km/h have been reached on the straight sections of the Cresta Run. Riders use their feet to help them steer and brake – special shoes with spiked toecaps are worn.

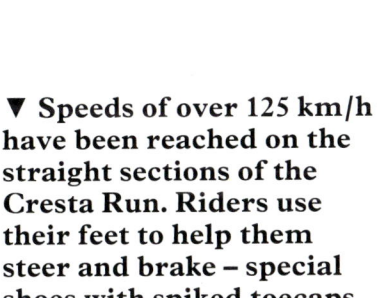

Cameras for the ski slopes

■ When you first go skiing, you'll probably be too busy trying to stay upright to worry about taking photos. It's always good to have souvenirs though, and professional photographers often visit ski classes to take shots of the groups. These are displayed later on, so you can choose the prints you want to order. To take your own photos, pick up some hints from this page.

▶ Keep your eyes open for unusual sights. Quick camera action captured this ski hang glider as it swooped over the slopes.

◀ A small automatic camera will fit safely inside a jacket pocket.
　If possible, fit an ultra-violet filter over the lens – this will stop the photos being too blue. Ultra-violet light from the Sun is very strong at high altitudes – it causes sunburn as well as affecting film.

▼ Some small all-in-one cameras even have built-in flash and zoom lens.

◀ Try and include some foreground interest to make your pictures a little different. Here a piste-maker frames a skier on a button lift.

36

◀ **Close-ups of family and friends are always better than long views dotted with tiny unrecognizable people. Action photos like this of a snowploughing beginner are best of all.**

Glossary

■ Here are explanations of some of the terms you'll read in this book – and hear when you go to the ski slopes.

Aerials
Acrobatic jumps off a ramp – a form of freestyle skiing.

Alpine skiing
Skiing down mountains, as opposed to cross-country or nordic skiing.

Ballet
A form of freestyle skiing, with similarities to ice-skating and gymnastics.

Bindings
The safety fittings that attach boot to ski – should be checked by an expert.

Black run
A steep and difficult piste which is suitable only for experienced skiers.

Blue run
At European ski resorts, an easy piste with a gentle slope suitable for beginners. Americans use this same colour for intermediate pistes.

Downhill
A high-speed race in alpine skiing.

Edges
The metal strips that run along the sides of skis.

Edging
Using body weight to put pressure on the skis' edges that are closest to the snow. This angles the edges into the snow and gives grip.

Egg position
Crouched racing position, used to streamline the body and increase speed by reducing air-resistance.

Fall line
The quickest and therefore steepest route from the top to the bottom of a slope.

Freestyle
A type of creative and acrobatic skiing – see aerials, ballet, and mogul skiing.

Gate
A ski race marker, made from poles and flags.

Green run
An easy piste, suitable for beginners. In Europe, these runs are even gentler than blue runs.

Herringbone
A way of climbing a hill – face uphill, with skis wedge-shaped, tips apart.

Hot-dogging
Another name for mogul skiing (see below).

Mogul
A bump or ridge on the snow, often caused by skiers turning on the same spot. Slopes that are too steep for piste-makers are often covered in moguls.

Mogul skiing
Freestylers use moguls to make spectacular turns and jumps. In competition, they ski down a set course to music, and points are given for style and technique, as well as speed.

Mono-skiing
Using one wide ski, feet positioned side by side, toes towards the ski tips.

Nordic skiing
Skiing across country, as opposed to downhill or alpine skiing. The term also includes ski-jumping.

Nursery slopes
Another name for the beginners' slopes, where the gradient is very gentle.

Off-piste
Areas of natural snow, which are not supervised or graded according to skiing ability – never ski these without a guide.

Parallel turn
Or parallel christie – an advanced turn, made with the skis side by side.

Piste
A prepared downhill ski trail, graded according to skiing ability.

Poles
Also called sticks or stocks – the metal-tipped poles used by skiers to balance, turn and push.

Red run
In Europe, an intermediate piste.

Schussing
Skiing downhill, with skis parallel to each other.

Sideslipping
Sliding sideways downhill, skis parallel and at right angles to the fall line.

Sidestepping
A way of climbing uphill taking one step at a time, skis parallel and at right angles to the fall line.

Slalom
A downhill race where skiers turn in and around gates. There are four slalom events. Giant and supergiant slalom are faster than ordinary slalom, and take place on longer courses. Parallel slalom is when two skiers race each other at the same time, on adjacent courses.

▲ Flying through the air with the greatest of ease – freestylers combine technique and skill with grace and extreme daring.

Snowplough
Gliding or turning with skis in a V or wedge, tips together, tails apart.

Stem turn
Or stem christie – this is an intermediary-level turn, between snowplough and parallel turns.

Traversing
Skiing across the fall line.

Weighted ski
The one carrying most of the skier's body weight.

39

Index

A
aeriels 30, 38
alpine skiing, *see* downhill skiing
Australia 24, 25
avalanche 21, 23

B
ballet 30, 38
bindings 8–9, 10, 38
black run 21, 38
blue run 21, 38
bobsleighs 34
body position 9
boots 7, 10
button lift 20, 36

C
cable car 20
cameras 36
chairlift 20
clothes 6, 10
competitions 25, 26, 28–29, 30, 34–35
Cresta Run 35
critical point 29
cross-country skiing 4, 10–11, 38
    competitions 25, 28–29

D
dog-sled racing 33
downhill skiing 4, 12, 14–15, 16, 18–19, 22, 24, 38
    races 25, 26–27

E
edges 8, 38
edging 13, 15, 16, 18, 38
egg position 22, 26, 38
equipment
    cross-country 10
    downhill 6–7, 8–9

F
falling 13, 19
fall line 14, 18, 19, 38

flying kilometre 26
France 25
freestyle skiing 30–31, 38
funicular railway 20

G
gates 25, 26, 38
giant slalom 26, 39
green run 21, 38

H
halfpipes 32
herringbone 13, 38
hot-dogging 38
history of skiing 24–25

I
in-run 29

K
kicker 30

L
lessons 12, 13
lifts 20–21
luge 34

M
moguls 38
mogul skiing 30, 38
mono-skiing 32, 38

N
nordic skiing, *see* cross-country skiing
norm point 29
Norway 24, 25
nursery slopes 13, 38

O
off-piste 38
Olympics, Winter 25
out-run 29

P
parallel turn 22, 39
photography 36–37

piste 17, 39
    signs 21
piste-maker 17, 36
poles 8, 13, 19, 22, 24, 29, 39

R
racing, *see* competitions
red run 21, 39

S
safety 20–21, 23
salopettes 6
schussing 12, 13, 14, 22, 39
shred 33
sideslipping 16, 39
sidestepping 13, 39
ski flying 29
skijoring 33
ski jumping 25, 28–29
ski pass 20
skis 8–9, 10, 24, 28
slalom 25, 26, 39
sledging 34–35
snowboarding 32
snowplough 14–15, 37, 39
    turn 18
sole, ski 8, 28
stem turn 19, 39
Switzerland 25, 35

T
table point 29
tail, ski 8
t-bar 20
telecabin 20, 21
tip, ski 8
traversing 16–17, 19, 39
turning 18–19, 22

U
unweighting 22

W
waxing 8, 10
World Championships 25
World Cup 25